D0963609

Understanding
Finance

Pocket Mentor Series

The *Pocket Mentor* Series offers immediate solutions to common challenges managers face on the job every day. Each book in the series is packed with handy tools, self-tests, and real-life examples to help you identify your strengths and weaknesses and hone critical skills. Whether you're at your desk, in a meeting, or on the road, these portable guides enable you to tackle the daily demands of your work with greater speed, savvy, and effectiveness.

Books in the series:

Leading Teams
Running Meetings
Managing Time
Managing Projects
Coaching People
Giving Feedback
Leading People
Negotiating Outcomes
Writing for Business
Giving Presentations
Understanding Finance
Dismissing an Employee

Understanding Finance

Expert Solutions to Everyday Challenges

Harvard Business School Publishing

Boston, Massachusetts

Copyright 2007 Harvard Business School Publishing Corporation

All rights reserved

Printed in the United States of America

11 10 09 08 07   5 4 3 2 1

No part of this publication may be reproduced, stored in or introduced into a re-
trieval system, or transmitted, in any form, or by any means (electronic, mechanical,
photocopying, recording, or otherwise), without the prior permission of the pub-
lisher. Requests for permission should be directed to permissions@hbsp.harvard.edu,
or mailed to Permissions, Harvard Business School Publishing, 60 Harvard Way,
Boston, Massachusetts 02163.

Library of Congress Cataloging-in-Publication Data

Understanding finance : expert solutions to everyday challenges.
    p. cm. — (Pocket mentor series)
  Includes bibliographical references.
  ISBN-13: 978-1-4221-1883-2 (pbk. : alk. paper)
  1. Finance. I. Harvard Business School Publishing Corporation.
  HG173.U53 2007
  658.15—dc22

                                    2007019484

The paper used in this publication meets the requirements of the American National
Standard for Permanence of Paper for Publications and Documents in Libraries and
Archives Z39.48-1992

Contents

The Budget Process   25

Four steps to developing an informed, effective budget.

What Is Cost/Benefit Analysis?   39

Techniques for determining whether to invest in a particular initiative.

Tracking Performance   55

Tactics for determining whether your investment is paying off.

Tips and Tools   61

Tools for Understanding Finance   63

Worksheets to help you create and track an annual budget, perform a breakeven analysis, and propose an initiative.

Test Yourself 67

A helpful review of concepts presented in this guide. Take it before and after you've read through the guide, to see how much you've learned.

Answers to test questions 70

Key Terms 73

Definitions of important and commonly used terms in finance.

To Learn More 89

Further titles of articles and books if you want to go more deeply into the topic.

Sources for Understanding Finance 93

Notes 95

For you to use as ideas come to mind.

Mentors' Message: Why Understand Finance?

No matter where you work in your organization, understanding basic financial concepts will help you do your job better and contribute to your company's efforts to stay in business and turn a profit.

Understanding Finance explains the basics of this important subject. It will not make you a finance expert, nor will it qualify you to become a financial analyst, controller, or chief financial officer (CFO). But it *will* explain what you need to know to be an intelligent consumer of financial information, to plan, and to use financial concepts in making business decisions.

Reduced to its essentials, business finance is about acquiring and allocating the resources a company needs to operate. Regarding resource *acquisition*, finance is concerned with questions such as:

- How will our company acquire and finance its inventory, equipment, and other physical assets?

- Should we use the owners' money, borrowed funds, or internally generated cash for resource acquisitions?

- How long does it take to collect money owed to us by customers?

And regarding resource *allocation*, finance helps managers answer questions like:

- If we could invest in several ventures, how might we determine which would ultimately generate the greatest value?

- What return must an investment produce to be worth making? And how should we measure return?

- How can we determine the profitability of our company's different offerings?

Sometimes finance is also part of a company's information system, along with accounting, to produce financial statements, budgets, and forecasts. These documents give you the numbers you need to ask key questions and to make savvy decisions for your own division, department, or team if you interpret and use them correctly.

Chuck Kremer, Mentor

Chuck Kremer, CPA, has many years' experience as an accountant, corporate controller, and business consultant. He is currently the senior business-literacy consultant with Novations VMS. He has helped thousands of nonfinancial executives overcome "fear of finance" using imaginative and enjoyable devices in Novations' *Financial Game for Decision Making* and *The Accounting Game* seminars. He is the lead coauthor of *Managing by the Numbers: A Commonsense Guide to Understanding and Using Your Company's Financials*. Chuck has developed *The Financial Scoreboard*, an Excel software template.

Karen Berman, Mentor

Karen Berman, PhD, is founder, president, and co-owner of the Business Literacy Institute, a consulting firm offering customized training programs, Money Maps, keynotes, and other products and services designed to ensure that everyone in organizations understands how financial success is measured and how they make an impact. Karen has worked with dozens of companies, from entrepreneurial firms to *Fortune* 500 organizations, helping them create financial literacy programs that transform employees, managers, and leaders into business partners. She is also coauthor, along with Joe Knight, of *Financial Intelligence: A Manager's Guide to Knowing What the Numbers Really Mean* (Harvard Business School Press, 2006).

Understanding Finance: The Basics

Understanding Financial Statements

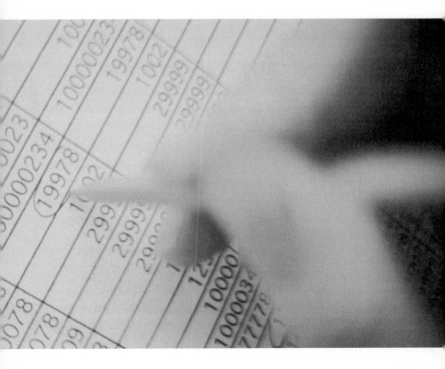

But it is pretty to see what money can do.
—Samuel Pepys

COMPANIES DO many things: build cars, process data, provide services, and even launch satellites. But the underlying purpose of all for-profit companies is to make money. As a for-profit manager, your job is to help the company make money—preferably, more money each year. Even if you work in the nonprofit or government sectors, where net income is neither the only nor the most important bottom line, it is still vital that you carefully monitor how much money comes in and where it gets spent.

You can help your company make money by reducing costs, increasing revenues, or both. You can also help the organization be financially successful by making good investments and using its assets to their fullest extent. The best managers don't just mind the budget—they look for the right combination of controlling costs, improving sales, and utilizing assets.

How's your company's financial health? Where does its revenue come from, and where does it spend its money? How much profit is it making? Where is its cash coming from, and where is it going to? Companies provide answers to such questions in three documents, called *financial statements*: the income statement, the balance sheet, and the cash flow statement. Publicly traded companies make these statements available to everyone—shareholders, industry analysts, and competitors as well. As a result, they are not as detailed as the company's internal financial statements.

Accounting methods

Financial statements follow the same general format from company to company. Depending on the nature of the company's business, however, specific line items may vary. Still, the statements are usually similar enough to allow you to compare one business's performance against another's. The reason for this similarity is that accountants abide by *generally accepted accounting principles*, or GAAP.

Most companies use *accrual accounting*: revenue and expenses are booked when they are incurred, regardless of when they are actually received or paid. This system relies on the matching principle, which helps companies understand the true causes and effects of business activities. Accordingly:

- Revenues are recognized during the period in which the sales activity occurred.

- Expenses are recognized in the same period as their associated revenues.

For example, at Amalgamated Hat Rack Company, which manufactures hat racks from imitation moose antlers, the revenue for a customer order is booked when each hat rack is sold—even if payment is made on account and the cash is not received immediately. Similarly, if Amalgamated receives two thousand brass hooks from a contracted supply company, those hooks are not all expensed at once. Rather, they are expensed on a per-unit basis: if it takes five brass hooks to make one hat rack, then the brass hooks are expensed five at a time as each hat rack is sold.

Occasionally, a very small company will begin its existence using *cash-basis accounting*, which counts transactions when cash actually changes hands. This practice is less conservative when it comes to expense recognition, but sometimes more conservative when it comes to revenue recognition. But as companies increase in size and complexity, it becomes more important to match revenues and expenses in the appropriate time periods, so they tend to switch over to accrual accounting.

The income statement

You might want to invest in a company for many reasons. Perhaps it's a leader in the industry. Or its CEO has a great record of turning companies around. Or its products are on the cutting edge of technology. But if the company is not turning a profit (otherwise known as net income or earnings), or it doesn't show strong potential to become profitable over the medium term, you probably wouldn't want to invest in it.

The *income statement* tells you whether the company is making a profit—that is, whether it has positive net income. (This is why the income statement is also called a profit and loss statement.) It shows a company's profitability for a specific period of time—typically, monthly, quarterly, and annually.

How does an income statement present this profitability picture? It starts with a company's revenue: how much money has come in the door from its operations. Various costs—from the costs of making and storing its goods, to depreciation of plant and equipment, to interest and taxes—are then subtracted from the revenue. The bottom line—what's left over—is the *net income* or profit.

Consider the example shown in the table "Income statement for Amalgamated Hat Rack." (Explanations for key terms follow.)

Income statement for Amalgamated Hat Rack

Retail sales	$2,200,000
Corporate sales	$1,000,000
Total revenue	**$3,200,000**
Cost of goods sold	$(1,600,000)
Gross profit	**$1,600,000**
Operating expenses	$(800,000)
Depreciation expense	$(42,500)
Operating income **(also called earnings before interest and taxes)**	**$ 757,500**
Interest expense	$(110,000)
Earnings before income tax	**$647,500**
Income tax	$(300,000)
Net income	**$347,500**

Source: Harvard ManageMentor® on Finance Essentials, adapted with permission.

The *cost of goods sold* is what it cost Amalgamated to manufacture the hat racks. It includes raw materials, such as fiberglass, as well as direct labor costs.

By subtracting the cost of goods sold from revenue, you get a company's *gross profit*—the profitability of the company's products or services.

Operating expenses include administrative employee salaries, rents, sales and marketing costs, as well as other costs of business not directly attributed to manufacturing a product. The fiberglass for making hat racks would not be included here; the cost of the advertising would.

Depreciation is a way of estimating the "consumption" of an asset over time. A computer, for example, might have a useful life of three years. Thus, according to the matching principle, the company would not expense the full value of the computer all in the first year of its purchase, but as it is actually used over a span of three years.

By subtracting operating expenses and depreciation from gross profit, you get *operating income*—often called *earnings before interest and taxes*, or *EBIT*.

Interest expense refers to the interest charged on loans a company takes out.

Income tax is levied by the government on corporate income.

BOTTOM LINE *n* **1:** net income (or profit), as shown on a company's income statement

---

The balance sheet

Most people go to a doctor once a year to get a checkup—a snapshot of their physical well-being at a particular time. Similarly, companies prepare *balance sheets* as a means of summarizing their financial positions at a given point in time.

Assets = liabilities + owners' equity

Assets are the things a company invests in so that it can conduct business—examples include financial instruments, land, buildings, and equipment. In order to acquire necessary assets, a company often borrows money from others or makes promises to pay others. That money, which is owed to creditors, is called *liabilities*. *Owners' equity*, also known as shareholders' equity, includes the capital that investors have provided and the profits retained by the company over time. If a company has $3 million in assets and $2 million in liabilities, it would have owners' equity of $1 million.

Assets	=	**Liabilities**	+	**Owners' equity**
$3,000,000	=	$2,000,000	+	$1,000,000

By contrast, a company with $3 million in assets and $4 million in liabilities would have negative equity of $1 million—and serious problems as well.

Thus, the balance sheet provides a description of how much, and where, the company has invested (its assets)—broken down into how much of this money comes from creditors (liabilities) and how much comes from stockholders (equity). Moreover, the balance sheet gives you an idea of how efficiently your company is utilizing its assets and how well it is managing its liabilities.

Balance sheet data is most helpful when it's compared with information from a previous year. In the table "Amalgamated Hat Rack balance sheet as of December 31, 2004," a comparison of the figures for 2004 against those for 2003 shows that Amalgamated has increased its total liabilities by $38,000 and increased its total assets by $38,000, thus resulting in no change in owners' equity. (Explanations for key terms follow.)

The balance sheet begins by listing the assets that are most easily converted to cash: cash on hand, receivables, and inventory. These are called *current assets*.

Next, the balance sheet tallies other assets that have value but are tougher to convert to cash—for example, buildings and equipment. These are called *fixed or long-term assets*.

Since most long-term assets, except land, depreciate over time, the company must also include accumulated depreciation in this part of the calculation. Gross property, plant, and equipment minus accumulated depreciation equals the current *book value* of property, plant, and equipment.

Tip: The balance sheet distinguishes between short-term liabilities, also known as current liabilities, and long-term liabilities. Short-term liabilities typically have to be paid in a year or less; they include short-term notes, salaries, income taxes, and accounts payable.

Amalgamated Hat Rack balance sheet as of December 31, 2004

	2004	2003	Increase/ (decrease)
Assets			
Cash and marketable securities	$355,000	$430,000	$(75,000)
Accounts receivable	$555,000	$512,000	$43,000
Inventory	$835,000	$755,000	$80,000
Prepaid expenses	$123,000	$98,000	$25,000
Total current assets	**$1,868,000**	**$1,795,000**	**$73,000**
Net property, plant, and equipment	$1,631,000	$1,666,000	$(35,000)
Total assets	**$3,499,000**	**$3,461,000**	**$38,000**
Liabilities and owners' equity			
Accounts payable	$440,000	$430,000	$10,000
Accrued expenses	$98,000	$77,000	$21,000
Income tax payable	$17,000	$9,000	$8,000
Short-term debt	$409,000	$500,000	$(91,000)
Total current liabilities	**$964,000**	**$1,016,000**	**$(52,000)**
Long-term debt	$750,000	$660,000	$90,000
Total liabilities	$1,714,000	$1,676,000	$38,000
Contributed capital	$850,000	$850,000	$0
Retained earnings	$935,000	$935,000	$0
Total owners' equity	**$1,785,000**	**$1,785,000**	**$0**
Total liabilities and owners' equity	**$3,499,000**	**$3,461,000**	**$38,000**

Source: Harvard ManageMentor® on Finance Essentials, adapted with permission.

Subtracting current liabilities from current assets gives you the company's *working capital*. Working capital gives you an idea of how much money the company has tied up in operating activities. Just how much is adequate for the company depends on the industry and the company's plans. For 2004, Amalgamated had $904,000 in working capital.

Most *long-term liabilities* are loans.

Owners' equity comprises *retained earnings* (net profits that accumulate in a company after any dividends are paid) and *contributed capital* (capital received in exchange for stock).

The cash flow statement

A *cash flow statement* gives you a peek into a company's checking account. Like a bank statement, it tells how much cash was on hand at the beginning of the period, and how much was on hand at the end of the period. It then describes how the company spent its cash.

If you're a manager in a large corporation, changes in the company's cash flow won't typically have an impact on your day-to-day functioning. But you can affect cash flow in your company. And it's a good idea to stay up to date with your company's cash flow projections, because they may come into play when you prepare your budget for the upcoming year. For example, if cash is tight, you will probably be asked to be conservative in your spending. Alternatively, if the company is flush with cash, you may have opportunities to make new investments.

If you're a manager in a small company, you're probably keenly aware of the firm's cash flow situation and feel its impact almost every day. The cash flow statement is useful because it shows whether your company is turning profits into cash—and that ability is ultimately what will keep your company solvent. As the example of Amalgamated Hat Rack continues, we see in the table "Amalgamated Hat Rack statement of cash flows, 2004" that the hat rack company generated cash flow of $95,500 in 2004. (Explanations for key terms follow.)

Amalgamated Hat Rack statement of cash flows, 2004

Net income	**$347,500**
Depreciation	$42,500
Accounts receivable	$(43,000)
Inventory	$(80,000)
Prepaid expenses	$(25,000)
Accounts payable	$20,000
Accrued expenses	$21,000
Income tax payable	$8,000
Cash flow from operations	**$291,000**
Property, plant, and equipment (PP&E)	$(7,500)
Cash flow from investing activities	**$(7,500)**
Short-term debt	$(91,000)
Long-term borrowings	$90,000
Contributed capital	$0
Cash dividends to stockholders	$187,000)
Cash flow from financing activities	**$(188,000)**
Increase in cash during year	**$95,500**

Source: Harvard ManageMentor® on Finance Essentials, adapted with permission.

The cash flow statement doesn't measure the same thing as the income statement. If there is no cash transaction, it cannot be reflected on a cash flow statement. Notice, however, that the cash flow statement starts with net income. Then, through a series of adjustments based on the increases and decreases in asset and liability accounts from the balance sheet, the cash flow statement translates this net income to cash.

In general, a company looks to three sources of cash: ongoing operations, investment activities, and financing activities. It's traditional to start with ongoing operations.

ACCOUNTS RECEIVABLE *n* **1.** The amount that customers owe the company for products and services sold but not yet paid for

---

ACCOUNTS PAYABLE *n* **1.** The amount the company owes its vendors for supplies and other items it has received but not yet paid for

---

Investment activities can be:

- Cash the company uses to invest in financial instruments or *property, plant, and equipment* (such investments in PP&E are often shown as *capital expenditures*)
- Proceeds from the sale of plant, property, or equipment
- Proceeds from converting its investments into cash

Financing activities include raising money by borrowing in the capital markets and issuing stock. *Dividends* must be paid out of cash flow; they represent a decrease in cash flow.

Using Financial Statements to Measure Financial Health

THE THREE FINANCIAL statements offer three different perspectives on your company's financial performance. That is, they tell three different but related stories about how well your company is doing financially.

- The *income statement* shows the bottom line: it indicates how much profit or loss a company generates over a period of time—a month, a quarter, or a year.

- The *balance sheet* shows a company's financial position at a specific point in time. That is, it gives a snapshot of the company's financial situation—its assets, liabilities, and equity—on a given day.

- The *cash flow statement* tells where the company's cash comes from and where it goes—in other words, the flow of cash in, through, and out of the company.

Another way to understand the interrelationships is as follows:

- The income statement tells you whether your company is making a profit.

- The balance sheet tells you how efficiently the company is utilizing its assets and how well it is managing its liabilities in pursuit of profits.

- The cash flow statement tells you whether the company is turning profits into cash.

By themselves, financial statements tell you quite a bit: how much profit the company made, where it spent its money, how large its debts are. But how do you *interpret* all the numbers these statements provide? For example, is the company's profit large or small? Is the level of debt healthy or not?

Ratio analysis provides a means of digging deeper into the information contained in the three financial statements. A financial ratio is two key numbers from a company's financial statements expressed in relation to each other. The ratios that follow are relevant across a wide spectrum of industries but are most meaningful when compared against the same measures for other companies in the same industry.

Profitability ratios

These measures evaluate a company's level of profitability by expressing sales and profits as a percentage of various other items.

- *Return on assets (ROA).* ROA provides a quantitative description of how well a company has invested in its assets.
  To calculate ROA, divide net income by total assets.

- *Return on equity (ROE).* ROE shows the return on the portion of the company's financing that is provided by owners.
  To calculate ROE, divide net income by owners' equity.

- *Return on sales (ROS).* Also known as net profit margin, ROS is a way to measure how sales translate into bottom-line profit. For example, if a company makes a profit of $10 for every $100 in sales, the ROS is 10/100, or 10 percent.
  To calculate ROS, divide net income by the revenue.

- *Gross profit margin.* A ratio that measures the percentage of *gross profit* relative to revenue, gross margin reflects the profitability of the company's products or services.

  To calculate gross margin, divide gross profit by revenue.

- *Earnings before interest and taxes (EBIT) margin.* Many analysts use this indicator, also known as *operating margin*, to see how profitable a company's operating activities are.

  To calculate EBIT margin, divide operating profit by revenue.

Operating ratios

By linking various income statement and balance sheet figures, these measures provide an assessment of a company's operating efficiency.

- *Asset turnover.* This shows how efficiently a company uses its assets.

Tip: To calculate asset turnover, divide revenue by total assets. The higher the number, the better.

- *Days receivables.* It's best to collect on receivables promptly. This measure tells you in concrete terms how long it actually takes a company to collect what it's owed. A company that takes forty-five days to collect its receivables will need significantly more working capital than one that takes four days to collect.

There are different methods to calculate days receivables. One way is to divide ending accounts receivable by revenue per day.

- **Days payables.** This measure tells you how many days it takes a company to pay its suppliers. The more days it takes, the longer a company has the cash to work with.

    There are different methods to calculate days payables. One way is to divide ending accounts payable by cost of goods sold per day.

- **Days inventory.** This is a measure of how long it takes a company to sell the average amount of inventory on hand during a given period of time. The longer it takes to sell the inventory, the more the company's cash gets tied up and the greater the likelihood that the inventory will not be sold at full value.

    To calculate days inventory, divide average inventory by cost of goods sold per day.

Liquidity ratios

Liquidity ratios tell you about a company's ability to meet its financial obligations, including debt, payroll, vendor payments, and so on.

- **Current ratio.** This is a prime measure of how solvent a company is. It's so popular with lenders that it's sometimes called the *banker's ratio*. Generally speaking, the higher the ratio, the better financial condition a company is in. A company that has $3.2 million in current assets and $1.2 million in current liabilities would have a current ratio of 2.7 to 1. That company would be generally healthier than one with a current ratio of 2.2 to 1.

To calculate the current ratio, divide total current assets by total current liabilities.

- *Quick ratio.* This ratio isn't faster to compute than any other—it simply measures the ratio of a company's assets that can be quickly liquidated and used to pay debts. Thus, it ignores inventory, which can be hard to liquidate (and if you do have to liquidate inventory quickly, you typically get less for it than you would otherwise). This ratio is sometimes called the *acid-test ratio* because it measures a company's ability to deal instantly with its liabilities.

  To calculate the quick ratio, divide current assets minus inventory by current liabilities.

Leverage ratios

Leverage ratios tell you how, and how extensively, a company uses debt. In the world of finance, the word *leverage* is used for debt.

- *Interest coverage.* This measures a company's margin of safety: how many times over the company can make its interest payments.

  To calculate interest coverage, divide income before interest and taxes by interest expense.

- *Debt to equity.* This measure provides a description of how well the company is making use of borrowed money to enhance the return on owners' equity.

    To calculate the debt-to-equity ratio, divide total liabilities by owners' equity.

Other ways to measure financial health

Beyond profitability, operating, and leverage ratios, other ways of evaluating the financial health of a company include valuation, Economic Value Added (EVA), and assessing growth and productivity. Like the ratios described above, all these measures are most meaningful when compared against the same measures for other companies in that particular industry.

Valuation. Valuation often refers to the process by which people determine the total value of a company for the purpose of selling it. This type of valuation is an uncertain science. For example, a firm that is considering acquiring another firm might rely heavily on estimates of future cash flows to come up with a value for the potential acquisition. Another firm might rely on different data. Also, a company is worth different amounts to different parties. For instance, a small, high-tech company may be valued more by a potential acquirer that wants the acquired firm's unique technology to leverage its other operations.

    Valuation also refers to the process that Wall Street investors and stock analysts use to scrutinize a company's financial statements and stock performance carefully in order to arrive at what they believe to be a realistic estimate of that company's value. Since a share of stock denotes ownership of a part of the company, analysts are interested in knowing whether the market price of that share is a good deal, relative to the underlying value of the piece of the company the share represents.

Wall Street uses various means of valuation—that is, of assessing a company's financial performance in relation to its stock price.

- The *earnings per share (EPS)* equals net income divided by the number of shares outstanding. This is one of the most commonly watched indicators of a company's financial performance. If it falls, it will likely take the stock's price down with it.

- The *price-to-earnings ratio (P/E)* is the current price of a share of stock divided by the previous twelve months' earnings per share. It is a common measure of how cheap or expensive a stock is, relative to earnings.

- *Growth indicators.* Growth measures can tell a great deal about financial health. A company's *growth* allows it to provide increasing returns to its shareholders and to provide opportunities for new and existing employees. The number of years over which you should measure growth will depend on the business cycle of the industry the company is in. A one-year growth figure for an oil company—an industry that typically has long business cycles—probably doesn't tell you very much. But a strong one-year growth figure for an

Internet company would be significant. Common measures of growth include sales growth, profitability growth, and growth in earnings per share.

Economic Value Added. This concept was introduced as a way to induce employees to think like shareholders and owners. It is the profit left over after the company has met the expectations of those who provided the capital.

Productivity measures. Sales-per-employee and net-income-per-employee measures link revenue and profit generation information to workforce data. Watching the trends of these numbers adds to your understanding of what is occurring in the company.

Tips: Analyzing Financial Statements

- Consider the context—what looks like a big (or small) number may not be once you understand what's typical for a business in that particular industry.
- Compare one company's statements with those of a similar-sized company within the same industry.
- Watch for trends. How have the statements changed since last year? From three years ago?
- Use your company's statements to write a paragraph that describes how much profit it is making, how well it is managing its assets, where the money comes from, and where it goes.

The Budget
Process

A BUDGET IS A blueprint for achieving specific goals. Your unit's budget is part of your company's overall strategy. So you need to understand your company's strategy in order to create a useful budget.

How can you familiarize yourself with your company's overall strategy?

- **Watch the overall economic picture.** A company's strategy during a recession will be far different than in a booming economy. Make a point to listen to your manager's and colleagues' views on sales and the economy—and make your own observations as well. Are you deluged by résumés, or is good help hard to find? Are prices rising or falling?

- **Stay on top of industry trends.** Even when the economy is booming, some sectors are going bust; your budget will need to reflect that reality.

- **Steep yourself in company values.** Every company has values, sometimes formalized and sometimes just "the way we do things." The very best companies keep those values in mind during every decision. Suppose your budget calls for a cut in the company's contribution to health-care plans. If the company's values view such cuts as anathema to its overall commitment to employees, your proposal will be dead on arrival.

- Conduct *SWOT analyses.* Every company has strengths, weaknesses, opportunities, and threats. Keep them in mind as you
  build your budget.

Understanding top-down and bottom-up budgeting

If your company does top-down budgeting, senior management
sets very specific objectives for such things as net income, profit
margins, and expenses. For instance, each department may be told
to hold expense increases to no more than 6 percent above last
year's levels. It's left up to you to allocate your budget within the
parameters to ensure that the objectives are achieved. For example, suppose Amalgamated Hat Rack decides that it wants to increase overall profitability by 10 percent. That could mean, among
other possibilities, launching a new product line to generate new
sales, or cutting overhead by upgrading technology, which would
reduce the need for part-time workers.

In addition, if your company does top-down budgeting, make
sure to look at the overall plans for sales and marketing, as well as
cost and expense plans, as you prepare your budget. The company's sales plan determines, to a large extent, how much money
will be available for the budget. The marketing budget will give
you an idea of what the company will be emphasizing in the coming year. Further, many companies strive to reduce expenses as a
percentage of revenue every year, no matter how slightly, as a way
to improve profitability.

In companies that do bottom-up budgeting, managers aren't
given specific targets. Instead, they begin by putting together budgets

What Would YOU Do?

Was the Budget on Track?

SIMONE WAS PLEASED. Recently promoted as manager of her company's human resource department, she had worked hard to develop the budget for her unit for the coming year. She had negotiated with management for the resources she needed, had made the assumptions behind her requests crystal clear, and had checked to be certain that her budget aligned with the company's strategy. But Simone also knew that preparing her budget and getting it approved were just the beginning steps in the budgeting process. As the coming year unfolded, she would have to find ways to assess whether the budget she had worked so hard to create was staying on track—or going off the rails. Though she understood the importance of tracking her budget, she felt somewhat uncertain about how to approach this responsibility.

that they feel will best meet the needs and goals of their respective departments. These budgets are then "rolled up" to create an overall company budget, which is then adjusted, with requests for changes being sent back down to the individual departments.

This process can go through multiple iterations. Often it means working closely with other departments that may be competing against yours for limited resources. It's best to be as cooperative as you can with other departments during this process, but that doesn't mean you shouldn't lobby aggressively for your own unit's needs.

Preparing a budget

As a manager, you are expected to put together a budget for your department each year. Your compensation may depend, to a large extent, on your ability to stick to that budget. So it's in your best interest to create a realistic budget when you start out. But don't sandbag either; it won't do you or your company any good.

Begin by setting goals. You may want to improve your division's performance over the previous year, increase net income for the company, or decrease costs—maybe even all three. How do you think your department can accomplish everything it has set out to do? That's where the budget comes into play. After all, a budget is a plan with numbers.

Start with a list of three to five goals that you'd like to achieve—and put a completion date on them, too. For example:

- Increase gross sales by 5 percent by June 30.

- Decrease administrative costs by 3 percent as a percentage of revenue by the end of the fiscal year.

- Reduce inventories by 2 percent by the end of the fiscal year.

Be sure you know the scope of the budget you're supposed to produce. Scope implies two things: the part of the company the budget is supposed to cover and the level of detail it should include.

- The smaller the unit that you're focusing on, the more you need to budget at the detail level. If you're creating a budget for a twelve-person sales office, you typically won't need to worry about such capital expenditures as major upgrades to the building or the computer equipment. But you should include estimates of what kinds of office supplies you'll need and how much they will cost.

- As you move up the organizational ladder to include more people and larger departments in your budgeting, your scope broadens. You can assume that the head of the twelve-person office has thought about paper clips and travel expenses. You're now looking at capital expenditures, studying the broad-brush outline and looking at how it all rolls up together.

Other issues to consider:

- **Term.** Is the budget just for this year, or the next five years? Most budgets are for the upcoming year, with quarterly or monthly reviews.

- **Overview.** Does your budget need to be accompanied by an overview of your strategic plan—for example, your plans for increasing sales or market share? If so, you need to be prepared to defend it.

Take a hard look at your assumptions for the coming year. After all, a budget, at its simplest, takes current data, adds assumptions,

Steps for Creating a Budget

1. Analyze your company's overall strategy.
2. If your company does top-down budgeting, start with the targets given to you by senior management. If your company does bottom-up budgeting, create these targets yourself.
3. Articulate your assumptions.
4. Quantify your assumptions.
5. Review: Do the numbers add up? Can you document your assumptions? Is your budget defensible?

and creates projections. Let's suppose you think sales will rise 10 percent in the coming year. If that's true, you may have to add two more people to your unit. But when you get before your budget committee, be prepared to defend your assumption that sales will rise 10 percent.

Role-playing may help you here. Put yourself in the position of a division manager with limited resources and many departmental requests for funding. How can you make your case for two additional staff members so that the division manager grants your request ahead of all the others?

Articulating your assumptions

The easiest way to get started is to take a look at your department's most recent budget. If you're the manager of Amalgamated Hat

Rack's Moose Head Division, you might decide to look at the 2005 budget (shown in the table "Moose Head Division, Amalgamated Hat Rack") to get ideas about how to increase revenues, cut costs—or both.

Moose Head Division, Amalgamated Hat Rack

2005 Budget	Budgeted	Actual	Variance
Sales by model			
Moose Antler Deluxe	$237,000	$208,560	$(28,440)
Moose Antler Standard	$320,225	$329,832	$9,607
Standard Upright	$437,525	$476,902	$39,377
Electro-Revolving	$125,000	$81,250	$(43,750)
Hall/Wall	$80,000	$70,400	$(9,600)
Total sales	**$1,199,750**	**$1,166,944**	**$(32,806)**
Cost of goods sold			
Direct labor	$75,925	$82,000	$(6,075)
Factory overhead	$5,694	$6,150	$(456)
Direct materials	$195,000	$191,100	$3,900
Total cost of goods sold	**$276,619**	**$279,250**	**$(2,631)**
Sales, general, and administrative costs			
Sales salaries	$300,000	$310,000	$(10,000)
Advertising expenses	$135,000	$140,000	$(5,000)
Miscellaneous selling expenses	$3,400	$2,500	$900
Office expenses	$88,000	$90,000	$(2,000)
Total SG&A	**$526,400**	**$542,500**	**$(16,100)**
Operating income	**$396,731**	**$345,194**	**$(51,537)**

Source: Harvard ManageMentor® on Finance Essentials, adapted with permission.

Don't start off by looking at specific revenue or cost line items, because revenues and costs are integrally linked. Instead, begin by asking yourself what events you want to see happen over the time frame you'll be budgeting for and what revenues and expenses are associated with each.

For example, do you expect to sell more products? How? If you plan to increase sales of your company's current products, there will be additional sales and marketing costs—maybe even new hires—associated with this strategy. Or if you intend to expand the company's product line, you will need to budget for a new product development initiative.

In the case of the Moose Head Division, the Standard Upright and Moose Antler Standard exceeded sales expectations in 2005. If these have the highest sales numbers, would it make sense to increase the sales projections for them, or should you stick with the 2005 sales volume for your 2006 projection? If you're looking to increase sales volume, the Standard Upright is a good choice: it beat its 2005 projection by 9 percent. Could you increase the anticipated sales for this model by 5 percent or 10 percent in 2006? In order to achieve this increase, how much more would you need to spend on marketing? To make the decisions, you'll also need pricing, market, and other relevant data.

Alternatively, do you expect to eliminate some products? At Amalgamated, the Electro-Revolving model is faring poorly. Would it be better to eliminate this line entirely and promote the newer Hall/Wall model? It would eliminate $81,250 in sales, but since the Electro-Revolving is very expensive to produce, perhaps the net result of discontinuation would not affect the bottom line very much.

Other questions to ask yourself include:

- Will you keep prices the same, lower them, or raise them? A price increase of 3 percent would have more than eliminated the budget's 2005 gross sales shortfall—provided that the increase did not dampen sales.

- Do you plan to enter new markets, target new customers, or use new sales strategies? How much additional revenue do you expect these efforts to bring in? How much will these initiatives cost?

- Will your salary expenses change? For example, do you plan to cut down on temporary help and replace these resources with full-time employees? Or will you be able to reduce salary costs through automation? If so, how much will it cost to automate?

- Are your suppliers likely to raise or lower prices? Are you planning to switch to lower-cost suppliers? Will there be a drop-off in quality? If so, how much will it affect your sales?

- Will your product have to be enhanced to keep your current customers?

- Do you need to train your staff?

- Are there other special projects or initiatives you are planning to pursue?

Quantifying your assumptions

Each of your assumptions and scenarios must be translated into dollar figures. If your entire staff of twelve needs sales training, you need to find out how much it will cost to train each person, and multiply that number by twelve to calculate the total cost. Some costs or revenues are easier to project than others—which is why it's always a good idea not to prepare your budget alone. Coworkers and direct reports will have valuable suggestions. Trade publications can often provide industry averages for a range of costs.

Once you've translated the assumptions into numbers, you need to incorporate those numbers into budget line items. Because your budget needs to be compared and combined with others, your company will probably provide you with a standard set of line items to use. In some cases, your quantified assumptions will constitute the entire line item—for example, you may have listed and quantified all the product development projects you'll be pursuing next year. In other cases, your assumptions will be incremental: if you plan to boost sales by raising prices, you'll start with last year's sales figures and then increase them by the appropriate amount.

Tip: As you put your budget into its required format, be sure to document your assumptions. It's easy to lose track during the translation, and you will want to be able to explain them—and revise them—when needed.

When you have compiled your budget, take a step back. Does the budget meet the goals that have been set for your unit? For example, if your goal was to increase gross sales by 5 percent, does the budget in fact do so? It's easy to overlook overall goals as you get into the line-by-line detail.

Furthermore, is your budget defensible? You may be perfectly happy with it, but not everyone else on the budget committee may be. Once again, you have to push your assumptions. Could you do as well with one extra staff member as with two? If not, be sure you can prove it.

Tips: Budgeting

- **Stay goal oriented.** If you aim to increase sales, make that the overriding concern of your budget. Don't let other issues sidetrack you from your main goal.
- **Be realistic.** Most new managers would like to double sales or cut expenses in half. But remember: you'll be held accountable for the results.
- **Don't try to do it alone.** Include your team members—they may have detailed knowledge about certain line items that you don't.
- **Don't use the budget as a substitute for regular communication with your staff.** Team members should hear directly from you about the funding for line items that affect them most directly— not by reading the finalized budget.
- **Don't blame denied requests on the budget.** Be direct: tell an employee if a requested business trip is unlikely to be worth the expense, instead of saying, "We just don't have money in the budget."

What You COULD Do.

Remember Simone and her need to track her budget for the HR department?

The mentors suggest this solution:

Simone needs to assess the performance of her budget at least monthly. In particular, she should pay special attention to large positive and negative variances, and figure out what's causing them. For example, a variance might be a one-time variation—in which case Simone wouldn't need to change anything. Still, she should keep monitoring such variances over subsequent months to make sure they do indeed straighten themselves out. If a variance *doesn't* represent a one-time aberration, Simone will need to assess why the variances are occurring and develop responses to them—which she could do by brainstorming ideas with her team.

In addition to tracking and addressing variances, she should also reassess forecasts quarterly as well as inform senior management if it looks as if she's not going to make her annual budget goals. That way, management can adjust the overall company forecast accordingly. Finally, Simone should also inform senior management if her unit's performance is turning out *better* than expected. And by saving her original budget assumptions and estimates, she'll be able to improve her budgeting ability for next year.

What Is Cost/Benefit Analysis?

COMPANY REVENUE

20   30   40

*The safest way to double
your money is to fold it over once
and put it in your pocket.*
—Frank McKinney Hubbard

A MALGAMATED RAT HACK is considering two investment options: buying a new piece of machinery and creating a new product line. The new machine is a plastic extruder
costing $100,000. Amalgamated hopes it will save time and money
over the long term, in addition to being safer than the current machinery. The second option, launching a line of coatracks, will re-
quire a $250,000 investment in plant, equipment, and design.

How does Amalgamated decide whether these investment options make economic sense?

The process of determining the answer is known as *cost/benefit
analysis*. Basically, this means evaluating whether, over a given
time frame, the benefits of the new investment or the new business
opportunity outweigh the associated costs.

Before you begin any cost/benefit analysis, it's important to understand the cost of the status quo. You want to weigh the relative
merits of each investment against the negative consequences, if
any, of not proceeding with the investment. Don't assume that the
costs of doing nothing are always high: in many cases, even when

significant benefits could be gained from a new investment, the cost of doing nothing is relatively low. (See the "Initiative Proposal Worksheet" in the Tips and Tools section.)

Steps of cost/benefit analysis

The cost/benefit analysis of a particular investment involves the following steps:

1. Identify all the costs of the new purchase or business opportunity.

2. Identify the benefits of additional revenues.

3. Identify the cost savings to be gained.

4. Map out the timeline for expected costs and anticipated revenues.

5. Evaluate the unquantifiable benefits and costs.

The first three steps are fairly straightforward. First, begin by identifying all the costs associated with the venture—this year's up-front costs as well as the ones you anticipate in subsequent years. Second, determine additional revenue that could come from more customers or from increased purchases from existing customers. To understand the benefits of these revenues, make sure to factor in the new expenses associated with them; ultimately, this means you'll be looking at profit. Third, cost savings can arise

What Would YOU Do?

The Case of the Frustrated Fortune-Teller

FRANÇOIS REALIZED MONTHS ago that his company needed to make significant inroads into the young-adult market. He made numerous presentations to senior management on new product concepts, market studies, and extensive competitive analysis. At the end of each presentation, he cautioned that if the company didn't move into this market soon, its competitors would beat the company to it. Finally, senior management said, "We need to understand the bottom line. Give us some projections." Projections? How could he confidently predict how much money the company would make at some future date? He wasn't a fortune-teller.

---

from a variety of sources; for the ones listed below, it isn't hard to quantify the savings.

- **More efficient processing.** This could mean that fewer people are required to do the processing, or that the process requires fewer steps, or even that the time spent on each step decreases.

- **More accurate processing.** The time required to correct errors and the number of lost customers could both decrease.

But be sure not to double-count cost savings in your expenses that go along with your additional revenue. Many times, the investment will either increase revenue or decrease expenses, but not both. So you'll do *either* step 2 *or* step 3.

In step 4, map out these two elements—the costs and the revenues or cost savings—over the relevant period of time. When do you expect the costs to be incurred? In what increments? When do you expect to receive the benefits (additional revenues or cost savings)? In what increments?

Once that's done, you're ready to begin the evaluation phase, using one or more of the following analytical tools:

- Net return (sometimes referred to as ROI)

- Payback period

- Breakeven analysis

- Net present value (NPV)

- Sensitivity analysis

Let's take a closer look at each of these tools.

Net return and payback period

Net return (sometimes called return on investment, or ROI) describes financial analysis of capital expenditures. To calculate net return, first subtract the total cost of the investment from the total benefits of the return. Then divide the net dollar amount of return by the total cost of the investment. This can help you compare returns on money your company spends internally with returns available elsewhere. However, because it does not address what is called the time value of money (to be addressed shortly), it does not provide the full picture.

Let's suppose that the new $100,000 plastic extruder Amalgamated is considering would enable the company to save $18,000 a year over the lifetime of the machine, which would be seven years. The total savings would thus be $126,000, making for a net dollar return of $26,000. Applying the formula—$26,000 divided by $100,000—the net return for the investment is a very attractive 26 percent.

But companies also want to know the *payback period*: how long it will take a particular investment to pay for itself. We already know that the plastic extruder is expected to save Amalgamated $18,000 a year. To determine the payback period, divide the total amount of the investment by the annual savings expected. In this case, $100,000 divided by $18,000 equals 5.56. In other words, the extruder will pay for itself in 5.56 years. The table "Amalgamated extruder savings" provides a year-by-year illustration.

Note that Amalgamated will not truly begin to reap the benefits of the investment for more than five years.

As analytical tools, net return and payback period have several benefits:

- They're easy to convey to upper management.
- They remind everyone that wise expenditures pay off financially.
- They adopt a long-term perspective.
- They help you compare different options.

Amalgamated extruder savings		
Year	Savings	Cumulative savings
1	$18,000	$18,000
2	$18,000	$36,000
3	$18,000	$54,000
4	$18,000	$72,000
5	$18,000	$90,000
6	$18,000	$108,000
7	$18,000	$126,000

Source: Harvard ManageMentor® on Finance Essentials, adapted with permission.

There is a drawback to both methods, however: they do not provide as accurate an economic picture as more sophisticated tools such as net present value and internal rate of return, because they ignore the time value of money.

Net present value and internal rate of return

These two analytical tools can be fairly complicated. Because most calculators and spreadsheet programs can make these calculations for you, we're only going to describe them broadly.

To begin, consider the principle that underlies both methods: the *time value of money*. In effect, this principle states that a dollar you receive today is worth more than a dollar you receive five years from today. The reason: even assuming no inflation, the dollar you receive today can be invested somewhere, which means that you will have more than a dollar by the fifth year.

Evaluating a new business opportunity means analyzing the income you expect that opportunity to provide at some point in the future. To perform that analysis, you'll be using a method for expressing future dollars in terms of current dollars. That's what *net present value* (NPV) and *internal rate of return* (IRR) calculations allow you to do.

Let's say that Amalgamated expects its new product line to start generating a cash flow of $60,000 annually, beginning one year from now and continuing for the succeeding five years. The questions for the company can thus be phrased as follows: given this expected cash flow stream and the $250,000 up-front cost required to produce it, is a new line of coatracks the most productive way to invest that initial $250,000? Or would Amalgamated be better off investing it in something else?

A net present value calculation begins answering these questions by recognizing that the $300,000 in cash flow that Amalgamated expects to receive over five years is not worth $300,000 in current dollars. Because of the time value of money, it is worth less than that. In other words, that future sum of $300,000 has to be *discounted* in order to be expressed accurately in today's dollars. *How much* it is discounted depends on the rate of return Amalgamated could reasonably expect to receive had it chosen to put the initial $250,000 investment into something other than the line of coatracks (but similar in risk) for the same period of time. This rate of return is often called the discount rate. In the Amalgamated example, assume a discount rate of 6 percent. The NPV function on your calculator or spreadsheet takes into consideration your initial investment, your yearly cash flow, your discount rate, and the time period (in years) that you are analyzing.

An NPV calculation determines the net present value of a series of cash flows according to the following algebraic formula:

$$\text{Net Present Value} = \text{Cash Flow (CF)}_0 + \frac{CF_1}{(1+i)^1} + \frac{CF_2}{(1+i)^2} + \frac{CF_n}{(1+i)^n}$$

where each CF is a future cash flow, n is the number of years over which the cash flow stream is expected to occur, and i is the desired rate of return, or the discount rate.

When you supply the values for each future cash flow, the discount rate, and the number of years, your spreadsheet or calculator will do the rest.

If the resulting NPV is a positive number, and no other investments are under consideration, the investment should be pursued. In the Amalgamated case, the NPV for the line of coatracks is $2,587, which suggests that it would be an attractive investment for Amalgamated. (Note: if the initial investment is made at the *end* of the first period, the NPV is $2,587. If the initial investment is made at the *beginning* of the first period, the NPV is $2,742. For the purposes of this example, we will use $2,587 as the NPV.)

But what about the other investment Amalgamated is considering, the $100,000 plastic extruder? At a discount rate of 6 percent, the NPV is $456, which is just barely positive. When we compare NPVs for the two investments—remember that the discount rate for each scenario is 6 percent—we see that both are positive, but the one for the coatracks is more positive. If Amalgamated could afford only one of these investments, therefore, it should go with the new line of coatracks.

Here, the effect that the discount rate has on the NPV should be emphasized. Suppose the discount rate were 10 percent instead of

6 percent: in that case, the NPV for the extruder would be $-11,244. The extruder would go from being a modestly attractive investment to being a very poor one.

Notice something else about the NPV calculation for the extruder: even with a 6 percent discount rate, the NPV is far less optimistic than the rosy 26 percent net return forecast. The point here is that although it's much more difficult to perform—and explain—the NPV analysis does result in more sophisticated, more comprehensive evaluations of investment opportunities.

Typically, when the *internal rate of return* is greater than the opportunity cost (the expected return on a comparable investment) of the capital required, the investment under consideration should be undertaken.

INTERNAL RATE OF RETURN (IRR) *n* **1.** A means for managers to decide whether to commit to a particular investment opportunity. IRR is the actual return provided by the projected cash flows. That rate of return can then be compared with the company's *hurdle rate*—the minimum rate of return that all investments for a particular enterprise must achieve.

The IRR calculation is based on the same algebraic formula as the NPV calculation. With the NPV calculation, you know the desired rate of return and are solving the equation for the net present value of the future cash flows. With IRR, by contrast, the net present value is set at zero, and the equation is solved for the rate of return. Your spreadsheet program or calculator will perform IRR calculations for you, just as it will for NPV.

What's a reasonable rate of return for a business to expect on an investment comparable to the one under consideration? Typically, it's well above what it could get on a risk-free investment, such as a Treasury bond. In many instances, companies will set a *hurdle rate*, a minimum rate of return that all investments are required to achieve. In such instances, the IRR of the investment under consideration must exceed the hurdle rate in order for the company to go forward with it.

If we return to Amalgamated's coatrack opportunity, the calculation yields an IRR for this investment of 6.4 percent, which is slightly above the discount rate of 6 percent. If Amalgamated's hurdle rate were 6 percent, it would go ahead with the new line of coatracks. But if the hurdle rate were 10 percent, the 6.4 percent IRR would mean that Amalgamated should not make the investment.

Breakeven analysis

Breakeven analysis is useful when considering an investment that will enable you to sell something new or to sell more of something you already make. It tells you how much (or how much more) you need to sell in order to pay for the fixed investment—in other words, at what point you will break even. With that information in hand, you can look at market demand and competitors' market shares to determine whether it's realistic to expect to sell that much. (See the "Breakeven Analysis Worksheet" in the Tips and Tools section.)

In more precise terms, the breakeven calculation helps you determine the volume level at which total contribution from a product line or an investment equals total fixed costs. But before you can perform the calculation, you need to understand the components that go into it.

- **Contribution** is defined as unit revenue minus variable costs per unit; it's the money available to contribute to paying fixed costs.

- **Fixed costs** are items such as insurance, management salaries, rent, and product development costs—they're items that stay pretty much the same no matter how many units of a product or service are sold.

- **Variable costs** are those expenses that change depending on how many units are produced and sold; examples would include labor, utility costs, and raw materials.

With these concepts, you can understand the calculation:

- Subtract the variable cost per unit from the unit revenue— this is the unit contribution.

- Divide total fixed costs, or the amount of the investment, by the unit contribution.

- The quotient is the breakeven volume, expressed as the number of units that must be sold in order for all fixed costs to be covered.

Consider the example of the new line of coatracks again. Suppose the new coatracks sell for $75, and the variable cost per unit is $22. The table "Breakeven calculation" shows how to determine the breakeven volume for the coatracks.

Breakeven calculation

$75	(unit revenue)
− 22	(variable cost per unit)
$53	(unit contribution)
$250,000	(total investment required)
÷ 53	(unit contribution)
4,717 coatracks (breakeven volume)	

Source: Harvard ManageMentor® on Finance Essentials, adapted with permission.

At this point, Amalgamated must decide whether the breakeven volume is achievable: is it realistic to expect to sell 4,717 additional coatracks, and if so, how quickly? To calculate the breakeven volume for the extruder, you would define the unit contribution as the cost savings per unit.

Sensitivity analysis

As noted earlier, Amalgamated would expect its new line of coatracks to begin generating $60,000 in annual profit beginning a year from now. But what if some variable in the scenario changed—how would it affect the overall evaluation of the investment opportunity? Sensitivity analysis enables you to ask just this kind of question and to see the ramifications of incremental changes in the assumptions that underlie a particular projection.

Sherman Peaboddy is the vice president of Amalgamated's Moose Head Division. He would exercise day-to-day oversight of the new product line, and he is the one projecting $60,000 in annual profit for five years. Natasha Rubskaya, the company's CFO, is more phlegmatic about the investment, primarily because she believes that Peaboddy has drastically underestimated the marketing costs necessary to support the new line. She predicts an annual profit stream of $45,000. Then there's Theodore Bullmoose, Amalgamated's senior vice president for new business development. Ever the optimist, he is convinced that the coatracks will practically sell themselves, producing an annual profit stream of $75,000 a year.

Amalgamated conducts a sensitivity analysis using the three different profit scenarios. The NPV for Peaboddy's is $2,587. For Rubskaya's, it's $–57,022. And for Bullmoose's scenario, the NPV is $62,196.

If Rubskaya is right, the coatracks won't be worth the investment. If either of the other two is right, however, the investment will be worthwhile—marginally so, according to Peaboddy's profit projections, and very much so, according to Bullmoose's. This is where judgment comes into play. If Natasha Rubskaya is the best estimator of the three, Amalgamated's board of directors might prefer to take her estimate of the coatrack line's profit potential. Better still, the company should analyze its marketing costs in greater detail.

Whichever route they take, the sensitivity analysis will give the board of directors a more nuanced view of the investment and how it would be affected by various changes in assumptions. Other contingencies, or changes in other variables, could be mapped out just as easily.

Estimating unquantifiable benefits and costs

The numbers don't tell the whole story, so your cost/benefit analysis should incorporate qualitative factors as well. Examples here include the strategic fit of the new opportunity with the company's mission, the ability to take on the new opportunity without losing focus, the likelihood of success given market conditions, and perhaps an increase in customer goodwill that the new investment would bring about.

- **Even though such factors are not fully quantifiable, try to quantify them as much as possible.** Make assumptions that can help you come up with a ballpark figure. Suppose you're trying to assess the value of improved information—more comprehensive data that is easier to understand and more widely available—that a new investment would bring. You could try to come up with a dollar figure that represents the value of employees' time saved by the new information or the value of the increased customer retention that might be gleaned from better understanding purchase patterns. Such estimates should not necessarily be incorporated into your ROI or NPV analysis, but they can be very persuasive nevertheless.

- **Weigh the quantifiable and the unquantifiable factors.** For example, if the net present value of an investment opportunity is only marginally positive, you may want to give more qualitative considerations, such as strategic fit, an equal weight in your final decision.

What You COULD Do.

Let's go back to François's problem of coming up with projections for making inroads into the young-adult market.

The mentors suggest this solution:

François might begin by performing a cost/benefit analysis on a particular product he has in mind for serving the young-adult market. A cost/benefit analysis identifies, over a given time frame, the costs and benefits of developing the product and then compares those figures to see whether launching the product makes economic sense. Once François has performed the cost/benefit analysis, he can further evaluate the proposed product's potential by using one or more of the following analytical tools: net return, payback period, breakeven analysis, net present value, and sensitivity analysis.

The information, or projections, that François gathers will help senior management understand the bottom line of the proposed product and determine whether the company should invest in it. For example, if François's various analyses indicate that the return on investing in the product doesn't meet his company's hurdle rate, then the firm may decide not to develop the product.

Tracking
Performance

COMPANY RES

Q 1

R EGARDLESS OF WHETHER you're tracking an investment opportunity you've decided to undertake or the annual budget you've created for your unit, you need to monitor your ongoing results to make sure your projections are on course. Just how closely you should keep tabs on the results depends on your level of management. If you're an office manager, you should be aware of how much you're spending on paper clips and travel costs; if you're a division manager, your focus is probably at a bigger-picture level.

Tracking the performance of an investment

When you evaluate a new investment, you're planning for the long term—typically a year or more. But in the real world, things change and plans go awry. And estimates are valid only for a limited period of time. Your first task, therefore, is to track your projections versus actual revenues and expenses. It's a good idea to do this on a monthly basis so that you can spot potential problems early on.

Consider the projections for the new Coatrack Division at Amalgamated Hat Rack. Management ended up using Theodore Bullmoose's optimistic profit projections. The table "Amalgamated Hat Rack, Coatrack Division, January 2007 results" shows the state of affairs early in the first quarter.

Amalgamated Hat Rack, Coatrack Division, January 2007 results

Item	Budget Jan.	Actual Jan.	Variance
Coatrack revenues	$39,000	$38,725	$(275)
Cost of goods sold	$19,500	$19,200	$(300)
Gross margin	$19,500	$19,525	$25
Marketing	$8,500	$10,100	$(1,600)
Administrative expense	$4,750	$4,320	$430
Total operating expense	$13,250	$14,420	$(1,170)
Operating profit	**$6,250**	**$5,105**	**$(1,145)**

Source: Harvard ManageMentor® on Finance Essentials, adapted with permission.

The division is doing reasonably well on revenues and cost of goods sold. Its only really large negative variance is in the marketing expense line. It's difficult to be certain based on just the first month's figures: is this simply a one-time, or seasonal, variation, or is Amalgamated going to have to spend more on marketing than Bullmoose had anticipated?

If your investment is not tracking according to budget, and if it looks as if the pattern of unexpectedly high costs (or unexpectedly low revenues) is going to hold, it may be necessary to rethink the initiative—or even to discontinue it. In the coatrack example, Amalgamated decides, after further investigation, that the higher-than-expected marketing costs will continue—and Bullmoose's prediction that the coatracks would sell themselves will not be borne out. The revised forecast, however, confirms Sherman Peaboddy's forecast about marketing costs and an annual profit stream of $60,000. The new line of coatracks still seems to be economically viable but not the huge success that Bullmoose believed it would be.

Tracking your budget

Tracking the budget for an already established unit involves many of the same procedures discussed above, but the continue-discontinue decision doesn't come into play as readily. Instead, managers monitor results in order to be able to make necessary spending or operating adjustments as quickly as possible. (See the "Annual Budgeting and Tracking Worksheet" in the Tips and Tools section.)

For line items that contain surprises, ask first whether the reason has to do with timing. In other words, do you have a monthly aberration or a long-term problem? If you suspect an aberration, you don't need to be too concerned—the situation should straighten itself out. Nevertheless, be sure to keep a close eye on those particular line items during subsequent months.

If the cause of the variance is not an aberration, however, you need to determine why the variances occurred. Then you should

---

Steps for Tracking Performance of an Investment

1. Assess monthly revenue performance versus budget.
2. Assess monthly expense performance versus budget.
3. Determine whether—and if so, how—your bottom line will be affected by any variances.

---

decide how you should respond as well as revise your forecasts, if necessary. Try to uncover what other reasons may lie beneath your faulty projections. Maybe expenses are higher than budgeted because sales have increased sharply—in which case, expense overruns would be good news rather than bad. In many cases, however, you'll have to try to find some way to make up the loss. Can you decrease spending for certain line items—to compensate for line items that are over budget?

Tip: Make sure to involve team members in figuring out how to address variances.

If it doesn't look as if you're going to make your budget, communicate this to upper management. That way, it can make appropriate adjustments in the overall company forecast. It may also provide you with direction on whether and how to address the shortfalls.

And last, reassess your forecasts quarterly. Budgets are made annually, but estimates are often inaccurate. It's not unusual to miss on your estimates from time to time. Reassessing quarterly is a good way to check your forecasts against reality. Updating your forecasts regularly ensures that you and senior management always have the latest and most accurate information to base decisions on.

But when you do adjust your forecasts, don't throw out the old estimates. When budget time rolls around next year, you'll want to be able to assess how accurate your original assumptions were. This will help you improve your estimates the next time around.

Tips and Tools

Tools for
Understanding Finance

UNDERSTANDING FINANCE

Annual Budgeting and Tracking Worksheet

Use this tool to prepare and track an annual budget with monthly or quarterly revenues and expenses. Enter your annual budget numbers on this sheet in the white cells. Use whole dollars for all entries. Monthly numbers will automatically be calculated on the "Enter Q1, Q2" and "Enter Q3, Q4" sheets that follow. If you would like to alter the monthly numbers in order to show timing of revenues or expenses, do so by simply overwriting the formulas in the monthly budget columns. Use the "Annual Budget Check" columns to make sure that you have not changed the annual totals by reallocating the monthly numbers.

Unit Name _____
Fiscal Year _____
Start Date of Year _January 1, 2005_

	Enter Annual Budget Here	Q1 Budget	Q1 Actual	Q2 Budget	Q2 Actual	Q3 Budget	Q3 Actual	Q4 Budget	Q4 Actual	YTD through Jun-07 Budget	YTD Actual	YTD Difference	YTD Percent Difference
Revenues													
Source 1		0	0	0	0	0	0	0	0	0	0	0	0%
Source 2		0	0	0	0	0	0	0	0	0	0	0	0%
Source 3		0	0	0	0	0	0	0	0	0	0	0	0%
Source 4		0	0	0	0	0	0	0	0	0	0	0	0%
Source 5		0	0	0	0	0	0	0	0	0	0	0	0%
Source 6		0	0	0	0	0	0	0	0	0	0	0	0%
Total Revenues	0	0	0	0	0	0	0	0	0	0	0	0	0%
Expenses													
Item 1		0	0	0	0	0	0	0	0	0	0	0	0%
Item 2		0	0	0	0	0	0	0	0	0	0	0	0%
Item 3		0	0	0	0	0	0	0	0	0	0	0	0%
Total Category 1	0	0	0	0	0	0	0	0	0	0	0	0	0%
Item 4		0	0	0	0	0	0	0	0	0	0	0	0%
Item 5		0	0	0	0	0	0	0	0	0	0	0	0%
Item 6		0	0	0	0	0	0	0	0	0	0	0	0%
Item 7		0	0	0	0	0	0	0	0	0	0	0	0%
Total Category 2	0	0	0	0	0	0	0	0	0	0	0	0	0%
Item 8		0	0	0	0	0	0	0	0	0	0	0	0%
Item 9		0	0	0	0	0	0	0	0	0	0	0	0%
Item 10		0	0	0	0	0	0	0	0	0	0	0	0%
Total Category 3	0	0	0	0	0	0	0	0	0	0	0	0	0%
Item 11		0	0	0	0	0	0	0	0	0	0	0	0%
Item 12		0	0	0	0	0	0	0	0	0	0	0	0%
Item 13		0	0	0	0	0	0	0	0	0	0	0	0%
Item 14		0	0	0	0	0	0	0	0	0	0	0	0%
Total Category 4	0	0	0	0	0	0	0	0	0	0	0	0	0%
Total Expenses	0	0	0	0	0	0	0	0	0	0	0	0	0%
Operating Income	0	0	0	0	0	0	0	0	0	0	0	0	0%
as a % of Revenue	0%	0	0	0	0	0	0	0	0	0	0		0%

Submitted by: _____   Date Updated: _____

UNDERSTANDING FINANCE

Breakeven Analysis Worksheet

Use this tool to determine a breakeven volume, the point at which total contribution equals fixed costs for your initiative. This will be calculated automatically as you enter your fixed costs, variable costs, and pricing information below.

Period: _____

Product: _____

Fixed Costs/Investment

Item 1
Item 2
Item 3
Item 4
Item 5
Item 6
Item 7
Item 8

Total Fixed Costs/Investment: $0.00

Notes:

Variable Costs per Unit

Item 1
Item 2
Item 3
Item 4
Item 5
Item 6
Item 7
Item 8

Total Fixed Costs/Investment: $0.00

Unit Revenue:
Unit Contribution:
Breakeven Volume/
Incremental Volume Required: $0.00

Initiative Proposal Worksheet

Use this form to develop a proposal for an investment or another initiative.

Initiative Name: **Date:**
Proposed By: **Status:**

Description of Initiative

Rationale for Initiative

Initiative Economics

Component	Amount	Description
One-time investment		
Annual costs		
Annual revenues		
Annual savings		
Return on investment		
Payback period		
Other		

Nonmonetary Costs	**Nonmonetary Benefits**
Component	Component

Risk Factors

Factor	How Managed

Initiative Schedule

Target start date: _____   Target completion date: _____

Timing rationale: _____

_____

Key Dates or Milestones	Deliverables	Key Dates or Milestones	Deliverables

Approved: _____   Date: _____

Test Yourself

This section offers ten multiple-choice questions to help you identify your baseline knowledge of finance essentials. Answers to the questions are given at the end of the test.

1. If you want to recognize revenue during the period in which the related sales activity occurred, which accounting method would you use?

    a. Accrual accounting.

    b. Cash-basis accounting.

2. Which of the following would be considered a cost of goods sold?

    a. Administrative employee salaries.

    b. Sales and marketing costs.

    c. Rents.

    d. Assembly labor costs.

    e. Advertising costs.

3. In most finance systems, what is the time frame that distinguishes short-term liabilities, also known as current liabilities, from long-term liabilities?

    a. Short-term liabilities typically have to be paid in a year or less; long-term liabilities take more than a year to repay.

    b. Short-term liabilities typically have to be paid within eighteen months; a long-term liability takes more than eighteen months to repay.

    c. Short-term liabilities typically must be paid in six months or less; long-term liabilities take over six months to repay.

4. If the income statement can tell you whether a company is making a profit, what does the cash flow statement tell you?

    a. How efficiently a company is using its assets.

    b. Whether a company is turning profits into cash.

    c. How well a company is managing its liabilities.

5. Many analysts like to look at a ratio that shows how profitable a company's operating activities are. Which ratio shows this?

    a. Acid-test ratio.

    b. Accounts receivable.

    c. EBIT margin.

6. At ABC Company, unit heads develop budgets for their departments that are linked to company performance objectives. Is this top-down or bottom-up budgeting?

a. Top-down.

b. Bottom-up.

7. As you begin to prepare your unit's budget, your manager reminds you to be aware of the "scope" of your budget. What does "scope" of a budget imply?

  a. The context of the proposed budget: the three to five goals that the budget you are going to prepare aims to achieve.

  b. The part of the company the budget is supposed to cover and the level of detail it should include.

  c. Whether the budget includes revenues and profits as well as the operating costs of your unit.

8. When you're preparing a cost/benefit analysis, net return and payback period analyses can help you compare and communicate the merits of different options. What, however, is the drawback to both analytic methods?

  a. Both net return and payback period analysis ignore the time value of money.

  b. Payback period and ROI do not take into account how long it will take for the investment to break even.

  c. ROI and payback period can only be used to evaluate potential capital investments, not other types of new business opportunities.

9. Your company is considering making an investment that could enable your division to sell more units of the Gargoyle tracking software introduced last year. Your manager has asked you to determine how likely it is that this investment will be recouped. What analytical method might give you this information?

    a. Sensitivity analysis.

    b. Breakeven analysis.

    c. Internal rate of return analysis (IRR).

10. To track your budget, you carry out three steps on a monthly basis. Step 2 is missing in the list below; what is it?

Step 1. Assess monthly revenue performance versus budget.

Step 2. _____

Step 3. Determine whether—and if so, how—your bottom line will be affected by any variances.

    a. Assess monthly expense performance versus budget.

    b. Assess monthly expense performance versus revenue performance for that same month.

    c. Compare monthly revenue performance with projected quarterly revenue performance.

Answers to test questions

1, a. With accrual accounting, income and expenses are recorded when they are incurred, regardless of whether cash is actually received or paid in that period. By matching revenues with expenses in the same time period, accrual accounting helps managers understand the true cause-and-effect connections between business activities.

2, d. Assembly labor costs are considered a "cost of goods sold." Cost of goods sold includes the materials, labor, and other expenses that are directly attributable to manufacturing a product or delivering a service.

3, a. Generally, short-term liabilities have to be paid in a year or less. Long-term liabilities stretch out over a longer time period and include items such as long-term bonds and mortgages.

4, b. It is the cash flow statement that tells you whether a company is turning its profits into cash.

5, c. Many analysts use the EBIT (earnings before interest and taxes) margin, often known as the operating margin, to see how profitable the company's operating activities are.

6, a. In top-down budgeting, senior management sets specific performance objectives for individual units. For instance, unit managers may be asked to limit expense growth to no more than 5 percent over last year's expenses. Unit managers then develop their budgets within those parameters to ensure that the high-level company objectives are achieved.

7, b. Scope implies two things: the part of the company your budget is supposed to cover and the level of detail it should include.

8, a. Because both methods ignore the time value of money, they do not provide as accurate an economic picture as more sophisticated tools, such as net present value and internal rate of return.

9, b. Breakeven analysis tells you how much (or how much more) of a product you need to sell in order to pay for a fixed investment—in other words, at what point you will financially break even. You can then use your sales history and knowledge of the market to determine whether the breakeven volume is achievable.

10, a. Step 2 is to assess the monthly expense performance versus budget. By understanding how revenue and expense performance compare against your budget, you can then determine whether (and how) your bottom line will be affected by any variances.

Key Terms

Accounts payable (A/P). Money owed by the firm to suppliers.

Accounts receivable (A/R). Money owed to a company for goods or services sold.

Accrual accounting. An accounting method whereby revenue and expenses are booked when they are incurred, regardless of when they are actually received or paid. Revenues are recognized during the period in which the sales activity occurred; expenses are recognized in the same period as their associated revenues.

Accruals. An amount incurred as an expense in a given accounting period—but not paid by the end of that period.

Acid-test ratio. See *quick ratio*.

Activity-based costing (ABC). An approach to cost accounting that focuses on the activities or cost drivers required to produce each product or provide each service. ABC assumes that most overhead costs are related to activities within the firm and that they vary with respect to the drivers of those activities.

Allocation. The process of spreading costs in a certain category to several cost line items, typically based on usage. For example, such corporate overhead expenses as rent and utilities may be charged to departmental units based on square feet.

Amortized expenses. The amount that is expensed over time for "soft" assets such as patents. They are expenses that are spread out over time to reflect their usable life.

Assets. The economic resources of a company. Assets commonly include cash, accounts receivable, notes receivable, inventories, land, buildings, machinery, equipment, and other investments.

Asset turnover. A measure of how efficiently a company uses its assets. To calculate asset turnover, divide sales by assets. The higher the number, the better.

Balance sheet. A means of summarizing a company's financial position—its assets, liabilities, and equity—at a specific point in time. According to the basic equation in a balance sheet, a company's assets equal its liabilities plus owners' equity. Balance sheet data is most helpful when compared with information from a previous year.

Banker's ratio. See *current ratio*.

Book value. The value at which an asset is carried on a balance sheet. The book value of equipment is reduced each year for depreciation. Therefore, the book value at any time is the cost minus accumulated depreciation.

Bottom-up budgeting. A process whereby managers put together budgets that they feel will best meet the needs and goals of their respective departments. These budgets are then "rolled up" to create an overall company budget, which is then adjusted, with requests for changes being sent back down to the individual departments.

Breakeven. The volume level at which the total contribution from a product line or an investment equals total fixed costs. To calculate the breakeven volume, subtract the variable cost per unit from the selling price to determine the unit contribution; then divide the total fixed costs by the unit contribution.

Capital expenditure/capital investment. The payment required to acquire or improve a capital asset. See *investment in PP&E.*

Cash-basis accounting. An accounting process that records transactions when cash actually changes hands. This practice is less conservative than accrual accounting when it comes to expense recognition, but sometimes more conservative when it comes to revenue recognition.

Cash flow statement. A review of a company's use of cash, this statement tells where the company's cash comes from and where it goes—in other words, the flow of cash in, through, and out of the company.

Chart of accounts. A way to outline a company's accounting system, the chart of accounts shows what information will be captured and what information will subsequently be readily retrievable by the system. The chart includes such items as inventory, fixed assets, accounts receivable, and costs.

Contributed capital. Capital received in exchange for stock.

Contribution. The unit revenue minus variable costs per unit. The sum of money available to contribute to paying fixed costs.

Cost/benefit analysis. A form of analysis that evaluates whether, over a given time frame, the benefits of the new investment or the new business opportunity outweigh the associated costs.

Cost of capital. The rate of return that a business could earn if it chose another investment with equivalent risk; also called opportunity cost.

Cost of goods sold (COGS). The costs directly associated with making and selling a product.

Cost of services (COS). The costs directly associated with developing and selling a service.

Costs and expenses. The costs related to running the business— for example, salaries, office overhead, light, heat, and legal and accounting services.

Current assets. Those assets that are most easily converted into cash: cash on hand, accounts receivable, and inventory.

Current ratio. This is a prime measure of how solvent a company is. It's so popular with lenders that it's sometimes called the *banker's ratio*. Generally speaking, the higher the ratio, the better financial condition a company is in. A company that has $3.2 million in current assets and $1.2 million in current liabilities would have a current ratio of 2.7 to 1. That company would be generally healthier than one with a current ratio of 2.2 to 1. To calculate the current ratio, divide total current assets by total current liabilities.

Days inventory. A measure of how long it takes a company to sell the average amount of inventory on hand during a given period of time. The longer it takes to sell the inventory, the greater the likelihood that it will not be sold at full value—and the greater the sum of cash that gets tied up. To calculate days inventory, divide average inventory by cost of goods sold per day.

Days payables. A measure that tells how many days it takes, on average, for a company to pay its suppliers. To calculate days payables, divide ending accounts payable by cost of goods sold per day.

Days receivables. A measure that tells you how long it takes, on average, for a company to collect what it is owed. A company that takes forty-five days to collect its receivables will need significantly more working capital than one that takes four days to collect. To calculate days receivables, divide ending accounts receivable by revenue per day.

Debt. What is owed to a creditor or supplier.

Debt to equity. This measure provides a description of how well the company is making use of borrowed money to enhance the return on owners' equity. To calculate the debt-to-equity ratio, divide total liabilities by total shareholders' equity.

Depreciation. A way of matching the cost of capital expenditures to the revenue it helps bring in.

Direct versus indirect costs. Costs that are directly attributable to the manufacture of a product—for example, the cost of plastic for a bottling company. Direct costs vary in direct proportion to the number of units produced. Indirect costs cannot be directly attributed to a particular product.

Dividend. A payment (usually occurring quarterly) to the stockholders of a company, as a return on their investment.

Earnings before interest and taxes (EBIT). See *operating profit*.

Earnings per share (EPS). One of the most commonly watched indicators of a company's financial performance, it equals net income divided by the number of shares outstanding. When EPS falls, it usually takes the stock's price down with it.

Earnings statement. See *income statement*.

Economic Value Added (EVA). The profit left over after a company has met the expectations of those who provided the capital.

Equity. The value of a company's assets minus its liabilities. On a balance sheet, equity is referred to as *shareholders' equity* or *owners' equity*.

Financial leverage. A company's long-term debt in relation to its capital structure (the total of its common stock, preferred stock, long-term debt, and retained earnings). A company that has consistently high earnings can afford to be more leveraged; that is, it can afford to carry more long-term debt than a company whose earnings fluctuate significantly.

Financial statements. Reports of a company's financial performance. The three basic types of statement included in an annual report—the *income statement*, the *balance sheet*, and the *cash flow statement*—present related information but provide different perspectives on a company's performance.

Fiscal periods. An accounting time period (month, quarter, year), at the end of which the books are closed and profit or loss is determined.

Fixed assets. Assets that are difficult to convert to cash—for example, buildings and equipment. Sometimes called long-term assets.

Fixed costs. Fixed costs remain constant despite sales volume; they include interest expense, rent, depreciation, and insurance expenses.

General ledger. A company's centralized and authoritative accounting record, where data included in the financial statements is detailed.

Generally accepted accounting principles (GAAP). The rules and conventions that accountants follow in recording and summarizing transactions and preparing financial statements.

Gross margin. A ratio that measures the percentage of gross profit relative to revenues.

Gross profit. The sum left over after you subtract COGS from revenue.

Growth. An increase in the company's revenues, profits, or the value of its equity.

Growth indicators. Measures that tell about a company's financial health. Common measures of growth include sales growth, profitability growth, and growth in earnings per share.

Hurdle rate. The rate of return on investment dollars required for a project to be worthwhile.

Income statement. A report that shows a company's revenue, expenses, and profit over a period of time—a month, a quarter, or a year. The income statement is also known as a profit and loss statement (P&L), statement of operations, and statement of earnings. It also can have the word *consolidated* in the title.

Interest coverage. This measures a company's margin of safety, or how many times over the company can make its interest payments. To calculate interest coverage, divide income before interest and taxes by interest expense.

Internal rate of return (IRR). The rate at which the net present value (NPV) of an investment equals zero.

Inventory. The assets of the company that are or will become its product. Examples include the merchandise in a shop, the finished work in a warehouse, work in progress, and raw materials.

Investment in PP&E. Dollars spent on property, plant, and equipment. Sometimes called *capital investment* or *capital expenditure.*

Invoice. A bill submitted to the purchaser, listing all items or services, together with amounts for each.

Journals. The transaction records of the business.

Leverage ratios. Ratios that tell you about a company's use of debt. These ratios, including *interest coverage* and *debt to equity*, help determine whether a company's level of debt is appropriate and assess its ability to pay the interest on its debts.

Liabilities. The economic claims against a company's resources. Such debts include bank loans, mortgages, and accounts payable.

Net book value (NBV). The value at which an asset appears on the books of an organization, minus any depreciation (usually as of the date of the last balance sheet) that has been applied since its purchase or its last valuation.

Net income. The profit of an organization after subtracting all expenses, including interest and taxes, from revenue.

Net income per employee. See *productivity measures*.

Net present value (NPV). The value of an investment, calculated by subtracting the cost of the investment from the present value of the investment's future earnings. Because of the time value of money, the investment's future earnings must be discounted in order to be expressed accurately in today's dollars.

Net profit margin. See *return on sales*.

Net return. A ratio measuring the value of the returns from an investment relative to its cost.

Operating cash flow (OCF). The net movement of funds from the operations side of a business, as opposed to cash from investing or cash from financing. OCF is usually described in terms of the sources and uses of cash. When more cash is going out than coming in, there is a negative cash flow; when more cash is coming in than going out, there is a positive cash flow.

Operating expenses. Expenses that occur in operating a business—for example, administrative employee salaries, rents, sales and marketing costs, as well as other costs of business not directly attributed to manufacturing a product.

Operating profit. The profit left over after subtracting the costs and expenses associated with conducting business from revenue. Also known as *earnings before interest and taxes (EBIT)*.

Operating ratios. Financial measures that link various income statement and balance sheet figures to provide an assessment of a company's operating efficiency. Examples of operating ratios include *asset turnover*, *days receivables*, *days payables*, and *days inventory*.

Owners' equity. See *equity*.

Payback period. The length of time needed to recoup the cost of a capital investment; the time that transpires before an investment pays for itself.

Pretax profit. Net income before federal income taxes.

Price-to-book ratio. A ratio comparing the market's valuation of a company to the value of that company as indicated on its financial statements.

Price-to-earnings ratio (P/E). A common measure of how cheap or expensive a stock is, relative to earnings. P/E equals the current price of a share of stock divided by the previous twelve months' earnings per share.

Productivity measures. Indicators such as sales per employee and net income per employee, which link revenue and profit generation information to workforce data, thereby providing a picture of which employees are producing the most sales and income.

Profitability ratios. Measures of a company's level of profitability, in which sales and profits are expressed as a percentage of various other items. Examples include *return on assets*, *return on equity*, and *return on sales*.

Property, plant, and equipment (PP&E) A line item on a balance sheet that lists the purchase price of the business's land, buildings, machinery, equipment, and natural resources that are used for the purpose of producing products or providing services.

Purchase order. A written authorization to a vendor to deliver goods or services at an agreed-upon price. When the supplier accepts the purchase order, it is a legally binding purchase contract.

Quick ratio. A measure of a company's assets that can be quickly liquidated and used to pay debts. It is sometimes called the *acid-test ratio*, because it measures a company's ability to deal instantly with its liabilities. To calculate the quick ratio, divide cash, receivables, and marketable securities by current liabilities.

Ratio analysis. A means of analyzing the information contained in the three financial statements, a financial ratio is two key numbers from a company's financial statements expressed in relation to each other. Ratios are most meaningful when compared with the same measures for other companies in the same industry.

Retained earnings. The total after-tax income that has been reinvested over the years of the business.

Return on assets (ROA). Expressed as a percentage, ROA is a quantitative description of how well a company has invested in its assets. To calculate it, divide the net income for a given time period by the total assets. The larger the ROA, the better a company is performing.

Return on equity (ROE)/return on owners' equity. This measure shows the return on the portion of the company's financing that is provided by owners. To calculate ROE, divide the total income by total owners' equity.

Return on sales (ROS). Also known as *net profit margin*, ROS is a way to measure a company's operational efficiency—how its sales translate into profit. To calculate ROS, divide net income by the total sales revenue.

Sales. An exchange of goods and services for money.

Shareholders' equity. See *equity*.

Sunk costs. Prior investment that cannot be affected by current decisions and thus should not be factored into the calculation of the profitability of an initiative.

SWOT analyses. An analysis of a company's strengths, weaknesses, opportunities, and threats.

Time value of money. The principle that a dollar received today is worth more than a dollar received at a given point in the future. Even without the effects of inflation, the dollar received today would be worth more because it could be invested immediately, thereby earning additional revenue.

Top-down budgeting. A budgeting process whereby senior management sets very specific objectives for such things as net income, profit margin, and expenses. Unit managers then allocate their budget within these parameters to ensure that the objectives are achieved.

Valuation. An estimate of a company's value, usually for the purposes of purchase and sale. Wall Street uses valuation to describe a company's financial performance in relation to its stock price: *earnings per share (EPS)*, *price-to-earnings ratio (P/E)*, and *price-to-book ratio*.

Variable costs. Costs that are incurred in relation to sales volume; examples include the cost of materials and sales commissions.

Working capital. A measure of a company's day-to-day liquidity, working capital equals the difference between a company's current assets (easily sellable goods, cash, and bank deposits) and its current liabilities (debt due in less than a year, interest payments, etc.). Shortages of working capital are often relieved by short-term loans.

To Learn More

Notes and Articles

Hawkins, David F., and Jacob Cohen. "The Balance Sheet." Note 9-101-108. Boston: Harvard Business School, 2001.

> Discusses the accounting equation and defines common terms found in the statement. Also provides an example of the balance sheets of Coca-Cola Co., Ariba, Inc., and Safeway, Inc.

Hawkins, David F., and Jacob Cohen. "The Statement of Cash Flows." Note 9-101-107. Boston: Harvard Business School, 2001.

> Discusses the components of the statement of cash flows and its direct and indirect format of presentation. Also briefly explains the difference between cash and accrual accounting and provides examples of Standard Microsystems Corp. and Intel Corp.

Kaplan, Robert S., and David P. Norton. "The Balanced Scorecard: Measures That Drive Performance." *Harvard Business Review* On-Point Enhanced Edition (2000).

> The balanced scorecard performance measurement system allows executives to view a company from several perspectives

simultaneously. The scorecard includes financial measures that reveal the results of actions already taken, as well as three sets of operational measures that assess customer satisfaction, internal processes, and the organization's ability to learn and improve.

Books

Berman, Karen, Joseph V. Knight, and John Case. *Financial Intelligence: A Manager's Guide to Knowing What the Numbers Really Mean.* Boston: Harvard Business School Press, 2006.

In *Financial Intelligence*, Berman, Knight, and Case teach the basics of finance—but with a twist. Financial reporting, they argue, is as much art as science. Because nobody can quantify everything, accountants always rely on estimates, assumptions, and judgment calls. Savvy managers need to know how those sources of possible bias can affect the financials and that sometimes the numbers can be challenged. While providing the foundation for a deep understanding of the financial side of business, the book also arms managers with practical strategies for improving their companies' performance—strategies, such as "managing the balance sheet," that are well understood by financial professionals but rarely shared with their nonfinancial colleagues. Accessible, jargon-free, and filled with entertaining stories of real companies, *Financial Intelligence* gives nonfinancial managers the financial knowledge and confidence for their everyday work.

Bruns, William J., Jr., Michael E. Edelson, Steve R. Foerster, W. Carl Kester, Timothy A. Luehrman, Scott P. Mason, David W. Mullins Jr., Andre F. Perold, and William A. Sahlman. *Finance for Managers*. Business Fundamentals Series. Boston: Harvard Business School Press, 1999.

This collection introduces managers to basic financial tools and concepts. Topics addressed include short- and long-term financial management, investment management, risk management, and valuation. It contains materials used in Harvard Business School's MBA and executive education programs. Includes the following items: "Note on the Financial Perspective: What Should Entrepreneurs Know?" by William A. Sahlman; "Note on Financial Programming Over Long Horizons" by Timothy A. Luehrman; "Introduction to Portfolio Theory" by Andre F. Perold; "Basic Capital Investment Analysis" by William J. Bruns Jr.; and "What's It Worth? A General Manager's Guide to Valuation" by Timothy A. Luehrman.

Jablonsky, Stephen F., and Noah P. Barsky. *The Manager's Guide to Financial Statement Analysis*. 2nd ed. New York: John Wiley & Sons, 2001.

This book is for nonfinancial managers who want to learn the language of business finance and accounting in order to become more effective in their jobs. Supplemented with several case studies of major corporations, the author explains how to get the most out of the complicated information provided in balance sheets, income statements, and other sections of the annual report, as well as in the *Wall Street Journal*, *Value Line*, and *BusinessWeek*.

Kaplan, Robert S., and David P. Norton. *The Strategy-Focused Organization: How Balanced Scorecard Companies Thrive in the New Business Environment*. Boston: Harvard Business School Press, 2000.

The creators of the revolutionary performance management tool called the Balanced Scorecard introduce a new approach that makes strategy a continuous process owned not just by top management, but by everyone. Kaplan and Norton articulate the five key principles required for building strategy-focused organizations: (1) translate the strategy into operational terms, (2) align the organization to the strategy, (3) make strategy everyone's everyday job, (4) make strategy a continual process, and (5) mobilize change through strong, effective leadership. The authors provide a detailed account of how a range of organizations in the private, public, and nonprofit sectors have deployed these principles to achieve breakthrough, sustainable performance improvements.

Sources for Understanding Finance

We would like to acknowledge the sources who aided in developing this topic.

Bruns, William J., Jr. "The Accounting Framework, Financial Statements, and Some Accounting Concepts." Note 9-193-028. Boston: Harvard Business School, 1993.

Bruns, William J., Jr. "A Brief Introduction to Cost Accounting." Note 9-192-068. Boston: Harvard Business School, 1993.

Bruns, William J., Jr. "Introduction to Financial Ratios and Financial Statement Analysis." Note 9-193-029. Boston: Harvard Business School, 1996.

Dickey, Terry. *The Basics of Budgeting.* Menlo Park, CA: Crisp Publications, 1992.

Hindle, Tim, chief contributor, and Alistair D. Williamson, ed. *Field Guide to Business Terms: A Glossary of Essential Tools and Concepts for Today's Manager.* The Economist Reference Series. Boston: Harvard Business School Press, 1993.

Livingstone, John Leslie, ed. *The Portable MBA in Finance and Accounting.* 2nd ed. New York: John Wiley & Sons, 1997.

Schleifer, Arthur, Jr. "Breakeven Analysis." Note 9-894-002. Boston: Harvard Business School, 1995.

Tracy, John A. *Budgeting à la Carte: Essential Tools for Harried Business Managers.* New York: John Wiley & Sons, 1996.

Tracy, John A. *The Fast Forward MBA in Finance.* New York: John Wiley & Sons, 1996.

Wilson, G. Peter. "Understanding the Statement of Cash Flows." Note 9-193-027. Boston: Harvard Business School, 1992.

Notes

Notes

Notes

Notes

Notes

How to Order

Harvard Business School Press publications are available world-wide from your local bookseller or online retailer.

You can also call:
1-800-668-6780

Our product consultants are available to help you 8:00 a.m.–6:00 p.m., Monday–Friday, Eastern Time. Outside the U.S. and Canada, call: 617-783-7450.

Please call about special discounts for quantities greater than ten.

You can order online at:
www.HBSPress.org